BANNACK

Foundation of Montana

Rick and Susie Graetz

Montana Fish, Wildlife & Parks

We thank the many folks who helped in the preparation of this work—Doug Monger, Ken Soderberg, Angie Hurley and Tom Lowe of the Montana Department of FWP, Brian Shovers of the Montana Historical Society, Vinola Squires and her staff of the Beaverhead County Museum Association and especially those who helped edit the manuscript.

Published by the Montana Department of Fish, Wildlife and Parks
Helena, Montana

Authored and photographed by Rick and Susie Graetz
Northern Rockies Publishing
Box 1707, Helena, Montana 59624
Thisismontana@aol.com

Book Design by GingerBee Creative
Helena, Montana

All color and prepress work done in Montana and Idaho, USA
Printed in Korea
ISBN 0-9753654-0-1

All photos by Rick and Susie Graetz unless otherwise noted.

A view of
Bannack from
the south.

Front Cover: Two of the social hot spots of Bannack the Hotel Meade and Skinner's Saloon. *Title Page:* Tom Lowe, Assistant Manager Bannack State Park, discusses Bannack's history with visitors Ms. Lewis and Ms. Clark. *Back Cover:* Tessa and Erin Hurley in period dress in front of the assay office.

FOREWORD

I first experienced Bannack more than twenty years ago. It was a quiet, fall evening. A sense of abandonment, mystery and untold stories lay heavily over the town. As my wife Cherie, daughter Amanda, good friend Billy Mack and I wandered the halls and rooms of the old Hotel Meade, our minds were filled with questions and our imaginations provided answers. Not knowing what we might find up a staircase or beyond a doorway, we hoped for insight into those who had once been a part of this place.

Today, I feel very fortunate to live and work at Bannack State Park. Sometimes, late at night when I walk the deserted streets, my imagination again runs wild. Who were the people that faced incredible hardships to arrive at this remote mining camp in the hopes of getting rich? A few prospered and achieved their dreams, while many struggle just to survive. Although much has been written about Sheriff Henry Plummer, the Road Agents and the Vigilantes, little has been recorded about the lives of the regular people who dreamed, worked, married, raised families and died in this remote but beautiful part of Montana.

What brought the first people to this isolated corner of Montana? Buffalo once thrived here. Before the white man, Indians lived on this land for thousands of years. Little is known about the first people, as they did not write in words. However, they did leave pictographs at numerous sites in the area, testament to their presence. The members of the Lewis and Clark Expedition were the first white people known to have seen this country and with the help of the Shoshone they were able to obtain horses and continue their journey to the Pacific Ocean. Although Lewis and Clark named today's Grasshopper Creek Willard Creek after Alexander Willard, a member of the expedition, by the time John White and his band of prospectors discovered gold in the creek the name had been long forgotten. Gold! The stuff dreams are made of. The early pioneers were following rumors of gold and chasing after treasure.

The story of Bannack is inextricably entwined with gold. If not for the presence of rich gold deposits along the creek and in the lode deposits in the surrounding mountains, Bannack would never have existed and today would most likely be part of a cattle ranch. The discovery of gold here in July of 1862 brought an influx of fortune seekers that swarmed over the hills and gulches in Montana. Bannack's population rose and fell with new discoveries and mining methods. The first, easily worked, placer deposits were soon exhausted. Different methods were used to extract the more difficult placer deposits and ditches and flumes were constructed to bring water to the "diggings." Later, in 1895, the invention of the world's first electric gold dredge brought renewed life to the town. Hard rock mining, although started in 1862, became more appealing with modern developments in mining and milling techniques. The beginning of World War II was the death knell for Bannack. All non-essential mining was prohibited and the mines and mills of Bannack fell silent. The town never recovered and thankfully Bannack became a State Park in 1954.

This book by Rick and Susie Graetz is the story of Bannack's beginnings as the first Territorial Capital of Montana. It has been my pleasure to work with Rick and Susie by showing them some of the places I know in this area and sharing what knowledge and insights I have about the town. Here is the long needed answer to some of the many questions about Bannack. I hope you will enjoy reading it as much as I have.

—TOM LOWE, Assistant Manager, Bannack State Park

3

Horse Prairie Valley and the Tendoy Mountains in the distance. The Corps of Discovery passed through here in the summers of 1805 and 1806.

BANNACK
FOUNDATION OF MONTANA

The town site of Bannack is a dot on the map, a mere speck in a vast sea of rugged mountains and broad valleys carpeted in sagebrush and bunchgrass. This corner of Montana remains relatively unspoiled, the terrain little changed since Lewis and Clark threaded their way toward the Continental Divide at Lemhi Pass, just west of Bannack.

Here, peaks soar to 11,000 feet and rivers and streams course through sloping "lowlands" at nearly 6,000 feet above sea level. Winter temperatures can dip to 50 degrees below zero, and summers are brief but glorious celebrations of greenery and the sound of running water. Trout and Arctic grayling rise to feed on a superabundance of mosquitoes and salmon flies, and elk forage undisturbed in high meadows.

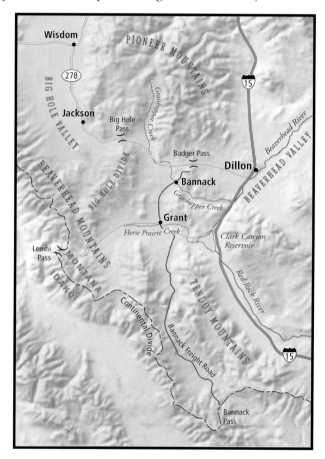

Even today the marks of civilization are dwarfed by the landscape. It's a 1,507-foot climb from downtown Bannack to the nearby 7,287-foot summit of Bannack Peak. From its top, long views extend 20 miles south to the Tendoy Mountains - named for a chief of the Bannock Indians - and 30 miles to the southwest to the 10,000-foot and higher peaks of the Beaverhead Range and the Continental Divide

Looking north just 15 miles distant, the rocky crags of the East and West Pioneers hold their heads aloft, topping out at 11,154-foot Tweedy Mountain. Closer in, a spacious saddle, draping from the flanks of 10,565-foot Baldy Mountain to the Rocky Hills, forms Badger Pass and carries Hwy 278 from the Beaverhead Valley and the Dillon area to the Grasshopper Creek Valley. The Rocky Hills are the mountains that cradle Bannack and concealed the desired gold.

Twenty-five eagle miles north of Bannack, near the outpost of Elkhorn Hot Springs, Grasshopper Creek gathers its waters from countless springs and creeks spilling out of the East and West Pioneers. The small waterway flows south traversing its namesake valley through idyllic ranch lands and sage covered hills before it knifes into a narrow canyon on the east edge of Bannack on its way to the Beaverhead River.

Grasshopper Creek
Valley near the
entrance to Bannack.

A beaver slide used
for stacking hay.
The Big Hole Divide
is on the left.

Bannack's western horizon is framed by the Big Hole Divide, a knobby ridge connecting the West Pioneers to the Beaverhead Range. Here, Hwy 278 crosses over Big Hole Pass down into the sprawling Big Hole Valley, legendary for fishing, haystacks, tough winters, and mosquitoes. During Bannack's heyday, the Big Hole—along with the Beaverhead and Grasshopper valleys—was the heart of Montana's emerging cattle industry. Some of the ranches still in operation grew from those early years and have been in the same family for generations.

The rugged terrain, harsh climate, and expansive ranching operations have sheltered the region from the more obtrusive inroads of human development. Today's vistas would not be unfamiliar to the area's first inhabitants.

NATIVE AMERICANS

Thousands of years before gold brought white men into this country, prehistoric people knew the area around Bannack. A quarry site in a gulch off of Horse Prairie Creek has been dated back 12,000 years, and archeologists have found medicine wheels and stone hunting points 8,000 to 10,000 years old. Of more recent vintage are tepee rings and bison jumps. Which tribes were first in Montana is up for debate—until Lewis and Clark's written journals in 1805 and 1806, history here was oral, passed down through generations, and one account often differed from another.

Sometime near the year 1700, the Shoshone Tribe came into Montana. Horses gave them an advantage over other tribes and allowed the Shoshone to dominate a wide territory extending from the far western reaches of the Bitterroot and Beaverhead mountains well out onto the high plains east of the northern Rockies. Then several bands of the Blackfeet Nation drifted to the Montana prairie from Canada. Acquiring horses and guns, they drove the Shoshone off the plains and into the high valleys along the Continental Divide.

Pushed into a smaller range, the Shoshone and their allies, the Bannocks and Sheepeaters, chose to live in the region that would become Idaho, crossing back over the passes of today's Beaverhead Mountains into the southwest province to hunt. With the exception of well-worn native trails and migratory camps, signs of human presence remained minimal; the Native Americans were light on the land. Soon though, all this would change.

LEWIS AND CLARK

The first known white men to reconnoiter the upper Beaverhead River were Lewis and Clark and the Corps of Discovery. As they struggled up the Beaverhead—which they called Jefferson's River—they were anxious for signs of the Shoshone. Sacajawea had assured the party her people would be friendly and would trade horses to help them over the high mountain passes of the Rockies. In mid-August 1805, nearly four months into their trek from Fort Mandan in the Dakotas, Meriwether Lewis noted information passed to him by William Clark that *at the distance a of 6 mi. by water they passed the entrance of a bold creek on Stard. side 10 yds wide ... which we call Willard's Creek after Alexander Willard one of our party.* More than 50 years later, the name would be changed to Grasshopper Creek.

Camping near the confluence of the Red Rock River and Horse Prairie Creek, where today's Clark Canyon Reservoir lies, the Corps named Horse Prairie Creek Valley "Shoshone Cove," and their campsite

"Camp Fortunate" for their luck in finding the Shoshone to trade for horses. On August 12, 1805, Meriwether Lewis ventured up Horse Prairie Creek and became the first known white person to cross Montana's Continental Divide when he stepped onto 7,373-foot Lemhi Pass in the Beaverhead Range.

In July 1806, after returning from the Pacific shores to their previous camp at Lolo Creek, the Corps of Discovery divided into two groups. Lewis stayed north, returning to the Great Falls of the Missouri by way of the Blackfoot River. Clark and his men retraced their route through the Bitterroot Valley before crossing into the Big Hole, which they christened Hot Springs Valley for the thermal springs at present-day Jackson.

Clark's party climbed out of the Big Hole Valley at today's Big Hole Pass and camped near the headwaters of Divide Creek. Recognizing the beginnings of a creek he had discovered the year before, he wrote *"some butifull Springs ... fall into Willards (Grasshopper) Creek ... I now take my leave of this butifull extensive vally which I call the hot spring Vally, and behold one less extensive and much more rugid on Willards Creek."*

On July 8, 1806, after following an Indian road down Divide Creek, Clark and his company turned south and trailed across the valley to Horse Prairie Creek where they *"proceeded on down the forke ... 9 Miles to our encampment of 17 Augt.* (1805, Camp Fortunate) *at which place we Sunk our Canoes & buried Some articles."*

The tranquility of the landscape the Corps of Discovery left behind in this part of the country had a very short future.

◄ Grasshopper Creek Valley.

▶ Looking toward the West Pioneer Mountains from Grasshopper Creek Valley.

Grasshopper
Creek Canyon
looking east
towards the area
where the first
"colors" were
found on July 28,
1862 by John
White and his
partners.

Lemhi Pass,
Meriwether Lewis
crossed here
Aug. 12, 1805.

Early-day artifacts
and remnants.

GRANVILLE STUART POINTS THE WAY

Fur trappers, following in the Corps of Discovery's footsteps, left no settlements in their wake. But it was a mere 50 years after Lewis and Clark, before prospectors were combing the West for gold. One man was instrumental in adding Montana to the gold-seekers' travel itinerary, and inadvertently setting events in motion that would lead to the settlement of Bannack and, eventually, Montana.

A twist of fate led Granville Stuart to the gold deposits in the country that was to become Montana. In 1857, Granville, his brother James, and cousin Reece Anderson were mining in Yreka, California, when they decided to return to Iowa to visit family. The trio commenced their eastward trek on July 14, 1857. They detoured north to avoid trouble in Utah, where Brigham Young had *"declared the state of Desert (Utah), free and independent of the United States."* When the group arrived at Malad Creek (south of today's Pocatello, Idaho), Granville became gravely ill and spent nearly two months recovering. Here he overheard rumors of possible placer gold near the Deer Lodge Valley in what was then Dakota Territory (seven years later to become Montana Territory).

On September 11, 1857, the group packed their bags and lit out north. Later, Stuart wrote in his book, *Prospecting for Gold*, *"We crossed to the Rocky Mountain Divide on the tenth day of October 1857, where the station called Monida is now ... As soon as we had crossed the Divide a wonderful change appeared in the country. Instead of the gray sagebrush covered plains of Snake river, we saw smooth rounded hills and sloping bench land covered with yellow bunch grass that waved in the wind like a field of grain. A beautiful little clear stream ran northwest on its way to join the*

Missouri river. This is now known as Red Rock Creek ... On the 24th of October we left Sage Creek and crossed the rather high ridge of Blacktail Deer Creek ... Having arrived at our destination, the Beaverhead Valley, we chose as a camping place a spot in the valley at the mouth of Blacktail Deer Creek (at its confluence with the Beaverhead River and about where Dillon is today—there were other people staying there as well) ... *We all lived in elk skin Indian lodges and were very comfortable ... Fifteen miles further down the Beaverhead at the mouth of the Stinking Water* (today's Ruby River) *was another camp of mountain men."*

One of those men was Robert Hereford, a trader on the various immigrant trails. Paul C. Phillips, who edited much of Stuart's works, surmised that it was Hereford who told Stuart of possible gold near Deer Lodge. While spending part of the winter in the Big Hole Valley, Stuart wrote, *"We resolved to go over to Deer Lodge where game was said to be abundant ... We were also actuated by a desire to investigate the reported finding of float gold by a Red River half-breed named Benetsee, in the lower end of Deer Lodge, 1852."*

On April 4, 1858, they moved to the Deer Lodge Valley and eventually joined up with Thomas Adams. On May 2, 1858, the Stuarts, Anderson, and Adams set out for Benetsee Creek (today's Gold Creek). Granville recorded, *"We followed it up the Creek about five miles carefully searching for any prospect or evidence of prospecting but found nothing. Near the bank of the Creek at the foot of the mountain we sunk a hole of about five feet deep and found ten cents in fine gold to the pan of sand and gravel. This convinced us that there were rich gold mines in this vicinity, but as we had no tools or provisions we could not do too much prospecting. This prospect hole dug by us was the first prospecting for gold done in what is now Montana and this is the account of the first real discovery of gold within the state."*

Being unprepared to work the area, they left the country and didn't return until the warm months of 1860, when they founded a small camp near Gold Creek, calling it American Fork (nothing is left of it today). Granville wrote to his other brother Thomas in Colorado, urging him to join them. Through that bit of correspondence, word got out to the "Pike's Peakers," as the Colorado prospectors were called, that this northern territory held gold.

Two years later, while aiming for Idaho, a Colorado party led by John White was prospecting its way through southwest Montana. Coming to Lewis and Clark's Willard Creek, they headed up its gulch to try their luck. On July 28, 1862, while panning the gravels of what they called Grasshopper Creek—owing to the dense population of "hoppers" on the its banks—the prospectors hit upon a bonanza. The place of discovery came to be called White's Bar and the "Grasshopper Diggings." Shortly, the sound of "Eureka!!" echoed through every mining camp in the west, setting off a genuine gold rush to Montana, and bringing a dramatic change throughout the southwest part of Big Sky Country.

Author Dorothy Johnson said, *"This was the best kind of a discovery ... free gold in the dirt and gravel of the streambed, gold that a man could wash out with crude equipment - with no more than the gold pan if that was all he had."* The strike was about three miles downstream from where the gold camp eventually sprouted, and early miners named their camp after a local tribe, the Bannock Indians. The spelling was inadvertently changed when the town's name was submitted to Washington, D.C, for the post office in 1862.

Grasshopper Creek in downtown Bannack.

An old wagon wheel most likely used on a stagecoach that traveled from Bannack to other towns in Montana Territory.

By the fall of 1862, up to 500 people had moved into Grasshopper Creek. As usual, the first to come claimed the most promising ground. It is estimated that by the time winter halted work, $700,000 worth of gold had been collected along the creek.

SOURCE OF THE GOLD

Dave Alt, author and professor of geology at the University of Montana, explains why gold was found in Grasshopper Creek and the surrounding gulches.

"At Bannack, as in many gold mining districts, much of the production came fast and early from bonanza deposits in stream placers. Early miners working the gravels in the streambed skimmed the cream off the district, leaving the hardest work and leanest pickings for those who came later. That happens because streams concentrate gold as though they were naturals sluice boxes. The process is really quite simple.

"When bedrock that contains gold, the so-called mother lode, breaks down into soil, the gold remains in the soil as flecks or nuggets of native metal. Then the process of erosion moves the soil down slope and dumps it, gold and all, into the stream. However, metallic gold is much denser than any other mineral and therefore tends to lag behind as the running water washes all the lighter minerals downstream. Occasionally, great floods that shift the entire streambed at once permit particles of gold to settle through the mass of moving gravel to the bedrock surface beneath. There they lodge against the irregularities, exactly as they do against the riffles in a sluice box."

The early gold miners weren't always satisfied with just a placer deposit. Many lived with the conviction that far greater wealth must exist in the bedrock. But in fact, bedrock deposits are generally much leaner than those in the streambed and more difficult to work. Bannack proved to be no exception.

At first glance, Bannack must have seemed an unlikely place to look for an ore body. The pebbles and boulders along the creek are limestone, a specimen that rarely contains gold. And since there is no gold upstream from Bannack, and very little downstream, the source of the bedrock gold must be within the cliffs above the area.

Geologists surmise that during a period of widespread volcanic activity in southwestern Montana, the limestone canyon walls on each side of Grasshopper Creek and a few hundred feet above its level were intruded by large masses of molten magma. The rock formed by the hardened magma was the most common igneous intrusion—granite.

When molten granite magma comes in contact with limestone, it reacts to create a wide variety of minerals. As the magma hardens, it forms an outside layer over the granite intrusion, separating it from the limestone. This mineral-filled contact zone may be anywhere from a few feet to a few hundred feet thick. Prospectors have long known that contact zones around granite intrusions, especially those in limestone, are likely to contain deposits of gold. The early miners at Bannack must have learned that lesson well. Before the summer of 1862 ended, they had found the gold in the contact zone and staked claims around its margins on both sides of Grasshopper Creek.

The Beaverhead
County Court-
house (left)
became the
Hotel Meade.
The A.F. Wright
Store (center)
was formerly
Skinner's Saloon.
The building
with the
Bannack Hotel
sign is actually
the Goodrich
Hotel and is no
longer standing.
**COURTESY BEAVERHEAD
COUNTY MUSEUM**

The first electric
gold dredge in
the United States
the "Fielding L.
Graves" in
Bannack 1895.
**COURTESY BEAVERHEAD
COUNTY MUSEUM**

Bannack in the 1860s.
MONTANA HISTORICAL
SOCIETY

General Merchandise
store in Bannack –
1860s.
COURTESY BEAVERHEAD
COUNTY MUSEUM

NOT FOR THE FAINT OF HEART

In early September 1862, freighters from Utah were heading for customers in the Deer Lodge Valley when they heard of this latest gold strike. Realizing they could shorten their trip and sell the goods in Bannack, they made an impromptu detour. This decision no doubt helped many of the miners survive the coming cold months.

When winter arrived, the camp wasn't exactly what could be labeled a town. Those who came first had no intention of staying. Get the gold and move onto another place was their motto. Few "buildings" had any semblance of permanency. Lean-to shelters, wikiups, tents, tepees, and a scattering of rudimentary cabins made up the "homes." The roads were a mass of mud after a rain or thaw. New provisions arrived erratically; wagon trains were often delayed by the weather.

That first winter was terribly cold. Early-day businessman Edwin Purple, in his memoirs stated, *"The weather during the fore part of winter was clear and cold; the labour of mining was carried on with difficulty. The pay dirt from the claims was heaped up in piles, upon which fires were built, and the water used in washing the earth was heated for that purpose. Up to the 1st of January 1863 little snow had fallen, but on that day a snowstorm which commenced during the night, covered the earth with thirty inches of snow. This suspended all mining operations except underground work for two or three weeks.*

"At this time the public places of resort were the saloons ... where lightening rod whiskey was sold at 25 cents per glass in gold dust. The demand for this article being great & the supply limited, the business soon played out, there being no way of replenishing the stock in trade."

Getting to Bannack from anywhere was an enormous effort. Those brave or desperate enough to chance fate not only had to contend with long distances over rugged terrain, and wild and unpredictable weather such as fierce blizzards and monumental snowstorms, but also with the Native Americans who were unhappy with this latest invasion by the white men. Emmet Nuckolls, in a letter published in the *Tri-Weekly Miner's Register* on December 26, 1862, warned, *"We are among the Bannock Indians here, but also the Snakes, Shoshones, Flat Heads and Blackfeet. These tribes are at war with each other all around us, and we know not how soon we will have to fight them. We expect it every day. They have killed 4 men here in the 1st three weeks ... I would not advise anyone, to come to this country yet. It may be rich in gold, but it is a very new country, and, for the Anglo-Saxon race, some trouble to keep the hair on your head."*

But life wasn't all danger and work, as Edwin Purple recalled. *"Balls and dancing were held two and three times a week ... These parties were pleasant and agreeable and patronized as they were by all the Ladies, married and single, did more to cultivate a spirit of good will ... among the citizens than all other means combined ... Order and decorum were strictly observed by all, and it never happened ... during the entire winter, that a rude or improper word was spoke ... Every body went in for a good time and they always had it."*

In his letters, Mr. Purple also tells the story of the first white child born in Bannack in December of 1862. The father of the newborn boy was a southern sympathizer and named the child Jefferson Davis. Two and one-half years later, as the fortune of the war had changed, he amended the toddler's name to Thomas Jefferson.

This now idyllic lot was once the backyard of the first governor's "mansion."

By spring 1863, 3,000 people found their way to Bannack. Another 2,000 were living up and down the gulch in four other settlements—Marysville, Bon Accord, New Jerusalem and Dogtown.

Civilization was coming to Bannack, as Edwin Purple relates, *"In April 1 (1863). C. Stickney was married to Miss Mary Kay Donnelly, who was during the winter one of the belles of Bannack, the other being Miss Matilda Dalton ... no clergyman could be found ... N. P. Langford who had acted as chaplain on Capt. Fisk's Train ... was therefore engaged for the purpose.*

"After the ceremony an elegant supper ... was partaken of, and dancing commenced which was kept up to a late hour. The guests were numerous, nearly everyone in town having been invited, and the occasion will long be remembered as the most elegant event of a social character, ever before had in Bannack, as well as for its being the first wedding ever celebrated in Montana Territory."

Granville Stuart felt Bannack was the place to be. But instead of digging for gold, he and his brother had its commercial possibilities on their minds. In November 1862, they arrived in town—James to open a store and Granville a meat business with the cattle he drove to Grasshopper Creek. Granville didn't stay long, though. By April 1863, he had closed his business, sold everything except some land and a couple of houses, and returned to the Deer Lodge Valley, which was more appealing to him.

GETTING THE GOODS TO BANNACK

Miners and prospectors weren't the only individuals drawn to Bannack. Like the Stuart brothers, others saw profits in providing goods and services. Less than a year after White's discovery, the main street was lined with saloons, stables, meat markets, general stores, two bakeries, and several hotels. Brothels, dance halls, a bowling alley, a Chinese restaurant, and a brewery added to the mix, as did doctors' and lawyers' offices. Tailors, carpenters, and blacksmiths were also part of economic development in Montana's first capital. This populace required not only the necessities of life, but also equipment and other provisions not available in the wilds of the northern Rockies. As a result, freighting became an important occupation. Owing to the mining camp's isolation and its distance from suppliers, it was expensive to live in Bannack.

For the first seven years, merchandise was shipped to Bannack one of three ways. Steamboats loaded with goods from St. Louis and points east plied the Missouri River as far as Fort Benton, where supplies were transferred to wagons that forged a 300-mile road to the town. Provisions also came overland from California to Lewiston, Idaho, then by pack string to the mining camp. Finally, land freighters made the long haul west from St. Louis to Salt Lake City.

To connect from Salt Lake City to Bannack, freighters blazed a rough 300-mile road across the prairie country of southeast Idaho. Near present-day Dubois, the road swung northwest along Medicine Lodge Creek and climbed to the wide, sagebrush-covered Bannack Pass and the Continental Divide. It then dropped into the Big Sheep Creek-Nicholia Creek Basin and continued north along yet another Medicine Lodge Creek on the west side of the Tendoy Mountains. The road cut through Horse Prairie Creek Valley (Lewis and Clark's Shoshone Cove) and ended with a steep descent into Bannack.

On May 10, 1869, the tracks of the Union Pacific and Central Pacific railways met at Promontory, Utah, the "golden spike" was driven, and the nation's transcontinental railway was completed. The nearby town of Corrine, Utah, 70 miles north of Salt Lake, grew as a transfer point for passengers and

▶▶ The first Masonic Lodge in Montana was built in 1874. The Masons met upstairs and school was held downstairs.

The road north from Bannack to Virginia City and points north. This now two-track road follows the old trail.

Big Sheep Creek and Nicholia Basin south of Bannack. The Bannack Freight Road heading to Bannack Pass and Salt Lake City passed through here.

A tour bus – Bannack style.

freight to be loaded onto wagons and stagecoaches headed to the gold camps and towns of Idaho and Montana. The time it now took to get to the Rockies from St. Louis was greatly diminished.

Traffic over Bannack Pass increased steadily as the freight road became a favored route. During the height of its life, within the 60-mile stretch between Bannack and the pass, five well-spaced stage stations provided food and shelter to travelers. By 1873 though, 11 years after its inception, use dwindled as the area's gold began playing out.

Today, the old wagon ruts of the Corrine-Bannack route can still be seen as they point southward up the hill out of Bannack. Modern-day explorers are able to trace the old road, most of which is now a well-maintained gravel and dirt county road (impassable in wet weather and snow-clogged in winter). Where the original trail crossed through the bottoms in Nicholia Basin, the route is yet visible. The county road somewhat parallels the old path, then rejoins it before reaching the Continental Divide.

Even more evident than the Corrine/Bannack Road is the main trail that led north to Virginia City, Helena, and other communities in the Territory. From the center of town up the east side of Hangman's Gulch, its well-worn markings are imprinted into the steep grade. About four miles from town, the route passes a formation known as "Road Agent Rock," the site of many holdups and other outlaw activity.

Bannack from
the rise above
the north side
of town.

SCHOOLS, CHURCHES, AND HIGHWAYMEN

In mid-September 1863, after traveling for more than three months by wagon from Omaha, Nebraska, a small party of weary travelers—newly appointed Idaho Chief Justice Sidney Edgerton (future Montana Territorial Governor), his wife Mary and their four children; Harriet and Wilbur Sanders (Mr. Edgerton's nephew) and their two children; Lucia Darling (Mr. Edgerton's niece); and Henry Tilden (another Edgerton nephew)—reached Bannack. Lucia Darling remarked of this event, *"we looked anxiously from the top of each ascent, hoping to see the longed for 'City' ... we at last halted on 'Salt Lake Hill' and looked down upon the little settlement along the banks of the Grasshopper. The view was not an inspiring one. There were a few log houses of diminutive size ... In the distance, the most conspicuous sight was the gallows, fitly erected near the graveyard in Hangman's gulch, just beyond the town."*

Harriet Sanders remembered her first impression was that *"Bannack looked to us most unattractive and uninviting ... I went at once with Mr. Sanders to take a look at what was to be our first home in the mountains, and I could hardly tell which was greater, my joy at leaving the wagon for a roof to cover our heads, or the disappointment I felt when I saw the room. The logs were still in the rough with the bark still on them, and Mother Earth for the floor ... our landlord considered to put a floor down ... Two bedrooms were improvised by hangings ... The kitchen was separated from the parlor and dining room by an imaginary partition ... My husband had two chairs made out of pine wood and canvas ... They were innocent of paint, springs or damask; but possessed the merit of comfort and durability ... When my carpet was down, and the furniture, which was most primitive, was placed, the room lined with muslin, and the lamp lit, we viewed the room with entire satisfaction."*

Weather that winter was wicked and made life challenging for the ill-prepared newcomers. According to a letter dated January 17, 1864, and written by Mrs. Edgerton, *"We had extremely cold weather here the week before last. The mercury in the thermometers after going forty degrees below zero froze in the bulb ... I was so afraid the children would freeze their ears or noses in the night that [I] got up a number of times ... to see that their heads were covered. Their beds would be covered with frost. I saw their frozen breath."*

For the most part, the streets and shops of Bannack were considered unsafe or unfit for genteel women. Because she was pregnant, and with her husband gone on business much of the time, Mary Edgerton rarely left her home. Her daughter Martha wrote how keeping up a house and caring for children allowed for little social time outside of the home. *"There were no labor-saving devices to lessen the task of the housewife ... Life was not easy for pioneer men, but the desirable element of excitement rendered it endurable, if not enjoyable. Pioneer women knew little save drudgery, and deprivation of most of the comforts to which they had been accustomed in the older, more civilized communities from which they came."* Martha Edgerton spoke of how since *"Men did most of the shopping, and nearly all of the gossiping ... the pioneer women missed the home folk more than the men, as they had no society or amusements to distract their minds."* She also stated, *"I could count on the fingers of one hand the number of women we knew in Bannack."*

Martha reminisced, *"Horse back rides, picnics, and berry picking excursions ... were the principle summer amusements of the women, while there was an occasional dance in the winter."*

Family
mementos.

Most houses
in town, like the
Stallings' cabin,
have their own
personality.

Other recent arrivals were also taken aback by conditions in Bannack. Mrs. Emily Meredith first set eyes on the town on September 6, 1862. After wintering over, she wrote to her father a less than reassuring letter, dated April 30, 1863. "*If I only had a house with a floor in it and a stove & I would consider myself quite fixed … I sometimes think, wonder what Mother would think if she could see my house. Rather rough living I guess, but most persons here would say I was quite comfortably settled.*

"*… many persons will undoubtedly come here this summer and make more than they could in years at home. And they ought to; a person ought to make money pretty fast here to pay them for living in such a place. I should like to see a pagoda or a mosque or anything to indicate there is a religious principle in man. If 'Labor is worship' this is a most worshipful community … I don't know how many deaths have occurred this winter, but that there have not been twice as many is entirely owing to the fact that drunken men do not shoot well … the bullets whiz around so, and no one thinks of punishing a man for shooting another.*"

Not many families dared to live in such an environment, but those who did were determined to see their children educated. In the summer of 1863, Mrs. Henry Zoller set up a "subscription school" in her home, charging parents $2 a week to teach their children. Unfortunately, Mrs. Zoller's tutelage lasted only two months.

In the fall of 1864, Lucia Darling brought to mind that, "*Bannack was tumultuous and rough, the headquarters of a band of highwaymen, and lawlessness and misrule seemed to be the prevailing spirit of the place. But into this little town had drifted many worthy people who unbendingly held*

Angie Hurley and her daughters Erin and Tessa patrol Main Street during Bannack Days.

Alter in the Masonic temple.

firmly to their principles of right. There were few families there and the parents were anxious to have their children in school." So she improvised a school in her uncle Sidney Edgerton's house; and as a record of its existence is available, it is considered as the first Montana public school. Twelve students attended the fall session. Christmas and rough winter weather ended the term until the arrival of spring. By the summer of 1864, the enrollment had increased substantially and a crude log cabin was built to accommodate the students. Schoolbooks were scarce and the only texts available were what the families brought with them.

Up until 1874, most schooling was carried out in various homes, stores and the rustic cabin. Then the education community and the organization of Masons joined to construct a two-story building for $1,500. School was taught on the ground level and the Masonic Order ensconced itself on the second floor. The school bell rang here for more than 70 years until 1951, when a dwindling student population forced closure.

This dual purpose building still stands with the distinctive Masonic Hall emblem—the square and compass—located at the peak of the front gable.

The problem of having a place to hold regular meetings wasn't restricted to the need for a school. Religion played an important part in the lives of the "respectable women," and they often remarked in their letters and diaries about the lack of a proper place to pray. Shortly after her arrival, Mary Edgerton wrote (in a letter dated October 18, 1863), "*It does not seem very much like Sunday here for they do not have any kind of meeting. There is no minister here except a Catholic minister.*"

The first jail built in Montana Territory - 1863 (right). The jail on the left was built in 1864.

Phyllis Friesen spins wool at Bannack Days.

NORTH

A. Parking Lot
B. Visitors Center
1. Yankee Flats
2. Governors mansion
3. Ryburn House
4. Masonic Lodge
   School house
5. Assay Office
6. Gibson houses
7. Hotel Meade
8. Goodrich Hotel
9. Chrismans Store

WEST

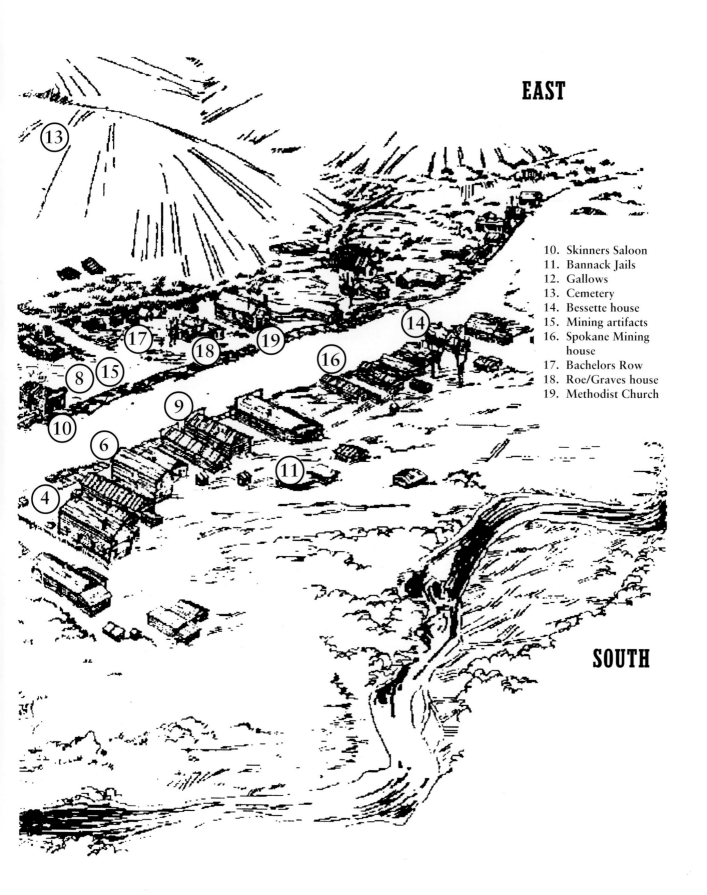

EAST

10. Skinners Saloon
11. Bannack Jails
12. Gallows
13. Cemetery
14. Bessette house
15. Mining artifacts
16. Spokane Mining house
17. Bachelors Row
18. Roe/Graves house
19. Methodist Church

33

SOUTH

34

The Methodist
Church built in
1877 under
the direction
of Methodist
missionary
"Brother Van."

Inside the Methodist
Church.

Early clerics who came to town were often found to be lacking in their ability to engage the faithful. On January 14, 1964, Lucia Darling wrote, *"Our preaching is done by a Methodist Exhorter and a Congregational minister ... Neither of them can preach, but we do what we can to keep up the meetings although there are few who attend them."*

Religious services improved when the affable Reverend George Smith showed up. *"I arrived in Bannack in June 1864 ... There was no Presbytery, no church, no Sabbath ... It was hard 'prospecting' in those days.*

"I was assigned to private apartments at the leading hotel ... in the office, with bar, gambling tables, gamblers, highwaymen, every man clothed in buckskin and adorned with a pair of navy revolvers and a bowie knife in the bootleg and Mexican spurs and dangles on the heel. My bed was the boardless floor of this public office, and bed clothing my blankets. This was the introduction to a life of strange vicissitudes and marvelous experiences. In some respects I was the most unfitted man in the world for such a life ... I was simple-hearted and true and believed everybody the same."

Bannack's high cost of living soon caught up with the reverend and it was necessary for him to *"seek more lowly quarters and humbler fare. I rented a log cabin 12X18 (feet) ... A storebox was table, cupboard and study desk and smaller boxes were chairs ... I paid $28 in my money for course factory sufficient to make a bed tick and pillow, which I filled with dried grass for a bed for myself and the mice that would steal a march on me and insist on bunking in with me. I did my own cooking, washing, ironing and mending ... and I got along magnificently.*

"I began preaching in an empty storeroom ... and I had the most intelligent and wide-a-wake congregation I have ever ministered unto."

Men who were determined to bring God's word to far-flung communities of Montana were not only devout, but also dependent on their own good humor. For six weeks in the summer of 1863, Bishop Daniel Tuttle of the Episcopal faith traveled more than 1,700 miles to visit 11 Montana towns, holding services in each and ministering to the parishioners. In a letter, he narrated a particularly memorable stopover, *"In Bannack scarcely any other religious services are ever held than my yearly ones. The Sunday I was there, the inhabitants thoughtfully suspended for once their customary weekly sports of horse-running, foot-racing, and cock-fighting, and came to the services."* An exceptionally large group of worshippers gathered in the second-floor room over one of the saloons. Not having been made to support a sizeable crowd, *"the floor gave way ... while we were singing the hymn before sermon. It sank four inches. We all expected to go utterly down. I am a great admirer of bravery, coolness, presence of mind, unselfishness; methinks I have pointed some rhetorical periods in commendation of these virtues. But the humiliating fact to be told is that when the floor gave forth that awful cracking, I was the first to spring out the door ... and down the stairs, in wild streaming robes. When my own feet were on 'terra firma' I was full of valuable courage ... and I shouted to the surging congregation: 'Don't rush, don't push, you'll break the stairs; you'll crush the children.' That kind and way of being courageous provokes a smile, doesn't it?"*

Ministers who "rode the circuit" became the norm for remote towns like Bannack. One such preacher who had a significant impact on the community was Methodist preacher William Van Orsdale.

Brother Van, as he was fondly called, arrived in Bannack at the peak of the mining activities and found all of the gambling houses and saloons open on Sunday. Stepping up to the bar in one of the

From l. to r.,
Crisman Store,
Ford's Saloon,
Gibson house,
Gibson boarding
house (later a hotel).

Ore cars used in
hard rock mining
in Bannack.

East end of Bannack
looking south.

drinking establishments, he announced himself as a minister. The bartender whistled the crowd to quietness and informed them that the bar would be closed for one hour. Brother Van had his chance and in his marvelous voice, sang the popular "Diamond in the Rough." The crowd, hungry for entertainment, called for more. The preacher continued and the "congregation" received a solid hour's worth of religion.

Van Orsdale proved to be a talented opportunist. In August 1877, Bannack had a major Indian scare. Chief Joseph and his Nez Perce nation had just defeated the US Army at the Battle of the Big Hole. Word had it that the Indians were heading for Bannack. Folks from around the area gathered in town to seek protection. The Indians never came, but they did kill four settlers in Horse Prairie to the south. The bodies were brought to the mining camp and buried by Brother Van.

After it was apparent the town was safe, Van Orsdale, being the promoter he was, took advantage of the large crowd present and talked them into building a real church. The Methodist Church, erected in 1877, was the first edifice in Bannack built exclusively for the purpose of worship and is one of the prominent structures on the east end of town.

Along with riches and business opportunities, there was also a darker side to the town's early days. Bannack, like most of the mining camps, was a rough and sometime dangerous place. Drunkenness, fights, robberies, killings, and the like were often the order of the day.

After spending time in San Quentin Prison in 1859, the infamous Henry Plummer came to town in the winter of 1862. Gaining the trust of the Bannack people, he was elected sheriff by the Miner's

Court on May 24, 1863. Immediately, Plummer organized 25 followers from his past into a gang named the Innocents, because they agreed to always plead their innocence in the unlikely event of their arrest. Under the protection of Sheriff Plummer, this band of vicious thugs set out to terrorize Bannack and other gold camps. In eight months, it is estimated they "legally" robbed and murdered more than 100 people.

In his book, Reminiscences of Four-Score Years, Judge Francis Thompson described the young Sheriff Henry Plummer. *"... when I saw him I could but wonder if this could be the young desperado whom people so much feared. He was about five feet ten inches in height, weighed perhaps one hundred and fifty pounds, and was, as Langford well says, 'In demeanor quiet and modest, free from swagger and bluster, dignified and graceful. He was intelligent and brilliant in conversation, a good judge of men, and his manners were those of a polished gentleman.'"*

Fear was widespread. Folks were afraid to travel and didn't feel safe in their homes. As the lawlessness increased and the jail remained empty, it soon became apparent to some that perhaps their sheriff was involved with the gang.

Mrs. Harriet Sanders writes, *"Henry Plummer desiring to be on good terms with the Chief Justice, Mr. Edgerton, and my husband, to prevent suspicion arising in their minds that he was engaging in the neferious occupation of brigandage ... invited Chief Justice Edgerton and wife, my husband and me to dinner on Thanksgiving day. Considering the meagerness of delicacies in the market and the extortionate prices charged, even for the necessities of life, the repast was one of the*

Winter here is often bitter but beautiful.
ANGIE HURLEY

The Bannack/ Hendricks Mill, constructed in 1917.

Quilter Betty Reynolds at Bannack Days.
COURTESY BANNACK ASSOCIATION

most sumptuous dinners I ever attended. Not only was the local market drawn on, but in carrying out his shrewed plans to quiet and evade the suspicion of his neighbors, he sent to Salt Lake City, a distance of five hundred miles, and everything that money could buy was served, delicately cooked with all the style that would characterize a banquette at 'Sharry's'. I now recall to mind that the turkey cost forty dollars in gold. The exceedingly high express charges then prevailing made turkeys in those days, expensive luxuries.

"I will describe Mr. Plummer as he impressed me that day. He was slender, gracefull and mild of speech. He had pleasing manners and fine address … the last person whom one would select as a daring highwayman and murderer."

Mrs. Edgerton also recalled the celebration in a letter to her sister, dated November 29, 1863, *"Lucia and Mr. Edgerton and myself had invitations to … an excellent supper equal to any that we ever had in Ohio. I tasted butter for the first time since we came here and it was a treat I can assure you, but as long as it is ten and twelve shillings a pound (and poor at that price) I think we shall do without it most of the time."*

On December 23, 1863, unwilling to be bullied and victimized any longer, the Vigilante Committee, consisting of regular citizens from both Virginia City and Bannack, was organized to stop the rampant terror and bring safety to the residents of the Montana Territory. Members were sworn in by Wilbur Sanders and Captain James Williams was their leader.

During the next 42 days, these self-authorized law enforcers went as far as the Hellgate in pursuit of members of Plummer's gang. Instead of orderly arrests, trials, and sentencings, the vigilantes took matters into their own hands and carried out a reign of lynching. By the end of January, they had executed 24 of the outlaws, including Henry Plummer, and banished or silenced the remainder.

Judge Francis Thompson had inadvertently been acquainted with Sheriff Plummer and many members of the Innocents and knew how dangerous and ruthless they were. In defense of the swift and seemingly unjust actions of the Vigilantes, the judge addressed their critics explaining, *"Far from the controls of any organized government, the people felt compelled in their might to rise and show the gamblers, robbers, and murderers, that they could no longer terrorize the people."*

To survive in these early days, many entrepreneurs found it necessary to be diverse and flexible in their business dealings. Martha Edgerton explained, *"Opposite our house lived George French, who kept a cabinet shop and carpenter shop, it was he who served as undertaker for Plummer, Ned, Ray, and Buck Stinson after their execution. Mr. French also owned a brewery, where the Cornishmen gathered on Saturday nights. Some of these had fine voices, and often our door stood ajar to hear the singing."*

Men and women alike were affected by the isolation of the town. Nathaniel Langford conceded *"Napoleon was not more of an exile on St. Helena than the newly arrived immigrant from the states in this recess of rocks and mountains."* Books and other reading materials were recycled from person to person. According to Langford, *"Old newspapers went the rounds of the camp until they literally dropped to pieces. Pamphlets, cheap publications, yellow covered literature … were in constant and increasing demand. Bibles … were read by men who probably never read them before."* Letters from friends and family were especially held dear. Mrs. Emily Meredith lamented to her mother, *"I have often felt as though I would willingly go without food for a week for the sake of a*

► Looking east
from the second
story of the
Hotel Meade.

40

The creek
that started
Montana's
goldrush in
July 1862.

letter from home ... I do not generally give way to homesickness although the life one leads here is enough to cause it." And Mary Edgerton wrote on December 27, 1863, *"We received letters from you week before last. You don't know how glad we were to hear from home. I have read them over and over."*

The familiar saying *"Neither snow, nor rain, nor heat, nor gloom of night stays these couriers from the swift completion of their appointed rounds,"* did not apply to the mail delivery of the mid-1800s. In a missive to her family back in Ohio dated January 1, 1864, Mary Edgerton chronicled, *"We received a package of letters from Lewiston today ... There were four from you dated June 14, Aug. 2, Aug. 16 and Sept. 8."* On June 4, 1864, Mary wrote to her sister, *"I received letters this morning ... mailed May 6th. You wonder that we don't get your letters sooner? We have lately got them in about a month after they were written. There was a time when the mails were very irregular because of the deep snow between this place and Salt Lake, but they are very regular now."* And at what price did these much anticipated communiqués appear? The average or usual cost seemed to be in the one-dollar range, but in 1862, Mrs. Emily Meredith related, *"While winter still reigned over a great part of the route a man came in with mail from Walla Walla. Through great hardship & at the risk of his life he brought them and they were eagerly received at $5.00 each by those to whom they were addressed."*

A NEW TERRITORY

The events leading to the creation of Montana as a Territory are carefully recounted in *Montana A History of Two Centuries*, by Michael P. Malone, Richard R. Roeder and William L. Lang.

"The advance of the mining frontier caused the eastern and western regions of Montana to be joined together in one political unit. In 1861-62, as miners began the rush into the newly opened goldfields of present-day north-central Idaho, settlers demanded a new territory in the Northern Rockies. Congress responded in March of 1863 by creating Idaho Territory. Carved out of Washington, Dakota, and Nebraska territories, Idaho embraced an enormous area, including all of present-day Idaho and Montana and most of Wyoming. Its capital lay on the far western border at Lewiston. Significantly, the creation of Idaho brought eastern and western Montana within a common boundary for the first time.

"Idaho Territory was a geographic impossibility. The massive ranges of the Rocky Mountains divided the territory in half, and a thousand miles separated Lewiston in the west from the far eastern extremities. Even in 1863, Idaho's population was shifting rapidly eastward, across the Continental Divide to the mining camps on the upper Missouri. With good reason, the Bannack-Virginia City miners believed that Lewiston—hundreds of miles away over endless, snow-clogged mountain passes—could never govern them properly. Miners began agitating for the creation of a new territory, to be split from Idaho along the crests of the Rockies.

"Fortunately for their cause, Judge Sidney Edgerton, the newly appointed chief justice of Idaho, arrived at Bannack in September 1863. Edgerton, a former Ohio congressman, was unable to proceed to Lewiston because of the approach of winter. He soon learned that the governor of Idaho had snubbed him by assigning him to the faraway judicial district lying east of the Divide. Both Edgerton and his nephew, Wilbur Fisk Sanders, took up the settlers' crusade to divide Idaho Territory. Edgerton

The site of many holdups, Road Agent Rock north of Bannack on the trail to Virginia City.

A sluice box used in placer mining sits in front of the Jackson house.

Tepees up
Hangman's
Gulch on
Bannack's
north side.

Doorways to
the past. Ford's
Saloon – late
1930s.

personally knew the president and many congressmen, so the miners chose to send him to Washington, D.C., to press their case. Carrying two thousand dollars in gold, Edgerton headed east in January 1864. Meanwhile, the Idaho legislature at Lewiston obligingly petitioned Congress to carve a new territory named Jefferson out of Idaho, with the dividing line along the Continental Divide and the 113th meridian, locating Idaho's new eastern boundary just west of the Deer Lodge Valley.

"Arriving in Washington, Edgerton consulted with President Lincoln and found him agreeable to the idea of a new territory in the Rockies. More important, Edgerton discovered that his friend and fellow Ohioan, Congressman James M. Ashley, had already begun work on a bill to form the new territory. Ashley, who chaired the House Committee on Territories, had the power to make his wishes felt. His political muscle and reports of the area's wealth of gold, which Edgerton reported as influential 'in such a mercenary age as ours,' pushed the bill speedily through Congress.

"While the bill lay in committee, Edgerton and his allies broke with the Idaho legislature by maneuvering the new territory's northwestern boundary three degrees to the west. This meant that the Idaho-Montana territorial line would generally follow the Bitterroot summits northward to the United States-Canada boundary and that Montana would take a 130-mile-wide bite out of northern Idaho. In this manner, Idaho lost the Flathead, upper Clark Fork, and middle Kootenai valleys to its new neighbor. The arrangement reduced the width of northern Idaho by three-fourths, leaving it an awkward 'panhandle,' cut off from the southern portion of the territory by the rugged Salmon River Mountains. Idaho petitioned Congress to restore these 'stolen' lands, but with no success. The Lewiston

Grasshopper Creek
in the Yankee Flats
area.

Window dressings

From the hills that
held the mother
lode and produced
the gold found in
and around
Bannack.

area even advocated establishing another territory named Columbia, which would join today's western Montana, northern Idaho, and eastern Washington, but the plan got nowhere. So, by circumstance and scheming, the new territory emerged with its jagged western border.

"The House and Senate also debated the name that Congressman Ashley had placed on his creation. 'Montana,' from the Latin or Spanish adjective meaning 'mountainous,' first appeared as a place name in 1858, when Josiah Hinman gave the name to a small mining town near Pike's Peak. Governor James William Denver of Kansas Territory remembered the name and suggested it to Senator Stephen A. Douglas as a name for a future territory in the Rockies. Ashley picked the name up from Douglas or somewhere else and liked it enormously. After trying unsuccessfully to give the name to what became Idaho in 1863, Ashley determined to apply it to Idaho's new neighbor.

"When Ashley's Montana bill reached the floor of the House, the Democrats began harassing the Republican about the name. The Democrats suggested dropping it and substituting the title 'Jefferson' to honor the founder of the Democratic Party or even 'Douglas' to commemorate the prominent Democratic senator from Illinois. Ashley and the Republicans would have none of it. Congressman Jacob Cox of Ohio suggested 'Shoshone,' but the name was scuttled when the Colorado delegate pointed out that Shoshone meant 'Snake,' a word that had unfortunate implications during the Civil War, when pro-Confederates from the North were called 'Copperheads.'

"Although Ashley won his battle in the House, two weeks later the Senate again challenged the name 'Montana.' Again, several members believed the classical name was inappropriate and argued

that an Indian word would be better. But no one could suggest a name with any relevance to the place, so they too settled on Ashley's title. Montana it became, and Montana it has remained. Following approval by Congress, President Lincoln signed into law the bill creating Montana Territory on May 26, 1864."

Edgerton's friendship with President Abraham Lincoln led to his appointment as the first Governor of Montana Territory on June 27, 1864. Facing the job of creating a government for the Territory, his first order of business was to name Bannack as the "capital." The choice was simple–Bannack was where Edgerton lived and he didn't want to move.

Politically, the Territory was a chaotic place with divisions within both political parties and entrenched feelings of pro-Union and Confederate sympathy widespread.

With the designation of the new Territory, a legislature was needed–another task for the governor. Clarke Spence, in his book *Territorial Politics and Government in Montana 1864–89*, lists Edgerton's challenges. *"His main concern was the infant Montana, a lusty but undisciplined babe, yet to be nurtured to political adulthood. It fell to Edgerton, as the first governor, to take the preliminary steps ... to breathe life into the machinery of self-government. From his office in a curtained-off corner of his log cabin, which also doubled as a residence and at times a schoolroom, the new chief executive outlined judicial districts, commissioned county officers, named Bannack as the temporary capital ... and ordered a census taken. Edgerton proceeded to establish districts from which members of the Legislative Council and House would be selected, and to call a general election for October 24, 1864, to elect not only these representatives, but a delegate to Congress as well."*

▲ Old Baldy in the East Pioneers from Grasshopper Creek Valley.

▸▸ The Grand Old Dame of the mining town.

Heavy snows often brought mining to a halt. The barn belonged to George French the local carpenter, cabinet maker, undertaker and brew master.

Lucia Darling, in a letter to her friends back east, was somewhat less impressed by these early political machinations. *"As far as the political prospects of the country* (Montana) *are concerned,"* she wrote, *"I cannot say they are very favorable but improving somewhat, it is thought ... Our election last fall ... sent a democratic candidate to Washington ... The man they have sent is a good representative of those who sent him, a man of small intellect but great bodily size, can swear and drink with the best (or worst) of them."*

Edgerton was a "radical" or "black Republican" as men of his leanings were called. That is, he was staunchly in favor of the preservation of the Union, wanted to see the south crushed, and advocated giving blacks voting rights. As a result, he was at odds with the Democrats who were in the majority in the state. As governor, he was fortunate to work with an evenly divided legislature. The Council was Republican by a single vote, and the House Democratic by the same margin.

At noon on December 12, 1864, Governor Sidney Edgerton presided over the 20 newly elected representatives in Bannack for the very first meeting of the Montana Territorial Legislature. After a joint session, the 13-member House reconvened in a two-story log building, and the 7-member Council (the future Senate) met in a smaller structure nearby. The precise location of the original "chambers" is not known, but early accounts place them in the vicinity of the Hotel Meade, which wasn't built until 1875.

In a letter dated January 12, 1865, Lucia Darling captured the demeanor of that first legislative assemblage. *"Our legislature met the 12th of Dec. ... It was feared at first the Copperheads would have a majority in both houses but it is nearly equally divided. One member ... could not take the oath as he had been in the rebel service. There was a great deal of swearing done before they would consent to take it but they were finally all sworn in except this one, he could not and would not take it so they fixed an oath for him and voted him in without ceremony ... Everyone was all excitement wondering ... if he* (the governor) *would recognize such a body or not. He informed the committee he had no communications to make until they were organized according to law and if they were going to admit members without taking the oath he should have nothing to do with them ... nor would they get any help from the government. The swearing before was faint in comparison to what they did now. They would never back down, but finally the troublesome member went home and then they said they would not meet in joint session to listen to the Governor's message, but they finally backed down on that too and the thing is moving quite quietly."*

Even as the historical first session was nearing a close, Bannack's political future looked bleak. The once easy-to-find gold was playing out and folks were leaving. On February 7, 1865, the lawmakers voted to move the capital to Virginia City, which grew out of the biggest gold strike ever in Montana at Alder Gulch on May 26, 1863. Virginia City retained first city status until April 19, 1875, when it too lost population and finally relinquished its title to Helena.

The newly minted legislators left Bannack to mixed reviews. They were inexperienced in the ways of governance, and given the tough conditions in the Territory, including a testy relationship with the Governor, probably did the best they could.

In his role as governor, Edgerton faced many difficult issues. The nation was involved in Civil War and on April 14, 1865, President Lincoln was assassinated. As a result, Montana wasn't on the nation's mind and much needed positions in the federal service weren't being filled. During the

This unusual style of picket was the fence of choice for homes in town.

Lobby of the Hotel Meade.

Territory's initial 16 months of existence, Montana had no Territorial Secretary who could sign federal warrants. This meant the governor could not spend federal funds. As a result, Edgerton, hoping to someday be reimbursed, paid for much of the cost of establishing a government out of his own pocket.

In late September 1865, a secretary finally arrived. Thomas Francis Meagher was appointed by Lincoln's successor, President Andrew Johnson, to be secretary of Montana Territory with an office in Virginia City.

Edgerton turned the reins of government over to the new Secretary, effectively making Meagher acting governor. Edgerton then left Bannack immediately to attend to personal business in Ohio and Montana concerns in Washington D.C. For whatever reason, before departing Bannack, the governor didn't request a leave of absence from the President. When he finally did make the request, it was refused and he was forced to resign his position. Had he asked for permission while in the Territorial Capital, it may have been granted, as his reasons for leaving were in Montana's interest. But President Johnson intensely disliked Republicans like Edgerton and seized this opportunity to get rid of him.

According to historian Clarke Spence, Edgerton *"could hardly be considered either an effective politician or a successful governor."* Yet considering the conditions he worked under—physically and politically–Edgerton's contribution seems enormous. Montana owes its size and name to the efforts of this gentleman from Ohio. Bannack would not have enjoyed its reign as first Territorial Capital and the distinction of serving as the foundation for the Territory and future state of Montana if Sidney Edgerton hadn't chosen it. Whatever followed in terms of government had its roots in the little mining camp on Grasshopper Creek.

The prominent Hotel Meade, often considered a symbol of Bannack, was originally built in 1875 to serve as Beaverhead County's first courthouse. In 1881, an election moved the seat to Dillon. This handsome red brick structure remained empty until 1890, when Dr. John Meade bought the deteriorating courthouse and remodeled it into a first-class hotel and dining establishment; it became the pride of Bannack's social life.

The hotel's continued success was ever tied to the fact that gold was still being extracted from the ground. When the shiny treasure played out, so did the glory days of the Meade. Sometime in the 1940s, as Bannack settled into disuse, the once vibrant Hotel Meade faded into history. Today, when folks walk its hallways and peer into the many rooms, some see or feel the presence of a young girl; most often she is sitting at the top of the curving stairway. This apparition is believed to be Dorothy Dunn, who drowned in Grasshopper Creek on August 4, 1916. Perhaps there is life still left in the old place.

The Big Hole
Valley and
snow-covered
Bitterroot Range
in the spring from
Big Hole Pass and
the Big Hole
Divide just west
of Bannack.

MINING MAKES A COMEBACK

Placer mining picked up again in the spring of 1866. Because water was needed to flush out the placer deposits, the first miners in the gulch ignored gravel that was too far from the creek. Now, ditches were built to extend the workings beyond the streambed. Prospectors could access more rich earth by sluicing the hillside and upper gulches.

Gold mining continued for several more years. But miners working manually couldn't reach the deposits on the bedrock, which were anywhere from 10 to 50 feet beneath the surface. A mere sluice box and shovel wouldn't do.

According to Dave Alt, "*During the spring of 1895, the first gold dredge in the United States, an electrically driven model, started work at Bannack. Another followed in the fall of the same year and two more machines arrived in 1896.*" Eventually, five dredges labored in Bannack.

A gold dredge sits on a barge and uses a long chain of steel buckets mounted on a conveyor belt to scoop the gravel bed of the stream down to bedrock. The gravel is then flushed through sluices to recover the gold, and the leftover gravel is dumped. As it bites its way along, the barge floats on a small lake of its own making. Ponds created by this method of mining are still visible on Bannack's south side. The landscape is covered with dredging piles of discarded rocks the miners "forgot" to reclaim.

It didn't take long for the dredges to remove most of the remaining deep placer gold from the Grasshopper Creek area. In some places bedrock was too deep even for the dredges to get to. Some rich deposits might still exist, out of reach, owing to the expense of recovering them.

▲ The old
Alburn house
with Bannack
Peak in the
background.

▸▸ The ravages
of time are
evident on the
door to the
Stallings' cabin.

From the ages on
the tombstones, few
folks lived a long
life in Bannack.

Once taken for
granted, many
household items
were luxuries to the
early women of
Bannack.

Although hard-rock mining continued to take place downstream from the town site, once the dredges ceased, the population dwindled again. Remnants of the mines and parts of the mills that crushed the ore out of the rock and earth still stand as silent reminders of Bannack's last fling at gold mining.

As the price of gold plummeted and the mines closed (during World War II all non-essential mining was prohibited), the town's stream of income dried up. By the late 1940s, most of the citizens were gone. No longer were there stores to buy groceries in, doctors to visit, a school to attend, or post office to pick up mail. Soon, Bannack was abandoned, and the first Territorial Capital of Montana gained ghost town status.

But this was not a place that would crumble and sink into the dust. Concerned folks in southwest Montana joined together to preserve what was left. Ray Herseth, Bannack State Park manager from 1972 to 1984, credits Elfreda Woodside, a very active and dedicated board member of the Beaverhead County Museum Association in Dillon, as being the historic mining town's main champion. She was instrumental in convincing the primary landowner to sell his property to the Museum.

Vinola Squires, current director of the Museum, recalls from the records, "*Chan Stallings, a long-time Bannack resident bought the Bannack real estate of the I. B. Haviland Mining Company at a public auction in Butte on September 25, 1953. He then offered to sell the property to the Beaverhead County Museum and on November 4, 1953, the transaction took place. On January 23, 1954, the Beaverhead County Museum Association transferred ownership of the land to the State of Montana for a public park, historical site and recreational area for the generous sum of $1.00. If the state had failed to follow through on the commitment, the title would have reverted back to the Association.*" Later in 1954, Bannack State Park was created.

Today, thanks to the leadership and caring of Montana Fish, Wildlife and Parks and the non-profit Bannack Association, more than 50 of the original buildings remain. This wonderful place is preserved for all to stroll the streets and linger on the doorsteps of our heritage.

Gold accented
wallpaper from the
Graves' house.

"If I only had a
house with a floor
in it and a stove
& I would consider
myself quite fixed."
– Mrs. Emily
Meredith 1863.